The Historical Geography Of World

Eric Erickson

Contents

Translator's Foreword

The Age of Geographical Discoveries (1400-1600) is a very special period in human history. In this two-century-old age, new continents were discovered, the world was traveled by the sea for the first time, trade began to be carried out on a world scale, overseas empires were established for the first time, and depending on all these, the accumulated or natural wealth of the newly discovered continents and regions was the economic, economic and economic wealth of another continent, Europe. commercial, scientific, technological etc. was transferred as a source for its development, and as a result, there have been developments whose effects have been reflected until today. Almost all major problems today have roots, in one degree or another, going back to the Age of Geographical Discovery. Thus, the scientific revolution, the development of capitalism,

It is Eric Erickson's work that provides rational and comprehensive explanations of this historical phase, based on the latest research, and reveals its special place in general human history. In this respect, it gains more importance especially in our country, where there are not many solid sources specific to the Age of Geographical Discoveries.

In his work, Erickson does not dwell much on the position of the Ottoman Empire at its height in the Age of Geographical Discovery. However, the reader will easily find the necessary clues on this subject from the author's few words about the Ottoman Empire and mostly from his analysis of the states that made the discoveries.

I believe that this small but massive work, with its scientific analysis methods and rich knowledge, will be one of the essential books for those who are interested in the history of science and technology, the history of economy, political and military history, and finally the great historical adventure of humanity.

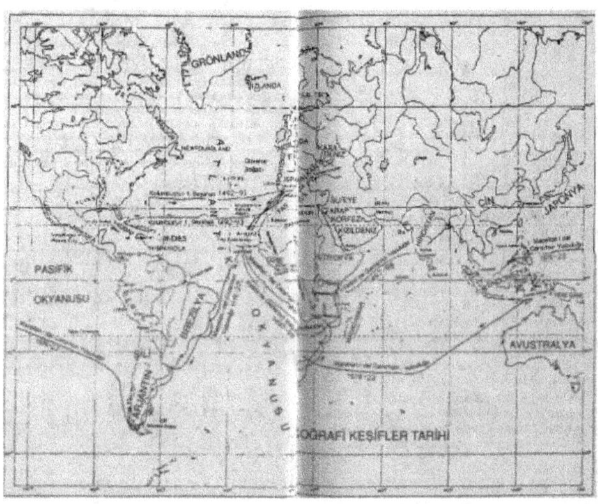

Login

In the 16th and 16th centuries, Europe's knowledge of the rest of the world underwent a fundamental transformation. In 1400, European maps were based only on guesswork, and the territories beyond their own coasts were often completely misrepresented on maps. Over the next 200 years, the continents drawn by European cartographers, like growing embryos, changed from obscure forms to the easily recognizable lines we are familiar with today. By 1600, only Australia, New Zealand, and the North Pacific remained as unmapped or missing places. Many of the most important discoveries were made in a short period of time. In the 30 years following Columbus' first crossing of the Atlantic in 1492, the Portuguese had returned to the Cape of Good Hope; They had advanced as far as China and Japan. 1521'

Indeed, long-distance travel and exploration were not new to the Arabs, Indians, Chinese, Vikings and Polynesians.

Before the 19th century Europeans, they had accomplished extraordinary ocean voyages. But these achievements of theirs were forgotten and were not repeated or were of no more than local significance. What is new in the Age of Discovery is that the world's oceans were connected to a single maritime system by means of geographical surveys, and the domination of these seas formed the basis for the eventual expansion of Europe's influence over every inhabited continent. The growth of Europe's geographic knowledge, the rapid expansion of

European trade and territorial control

followed. By 1600 Portugal had established a maritime empire stretching from Brazil and West Africa to the China Sea. Spain's American empire stretched from Texas to Chile, and other Europeans (Dutch, British, and French) openly coveted this commercial wealth and dominance of the Iberians.

How can we explain this rapidity and expansion of European geographical research? Was the Age of Discovery really as sudden and extensive as it seemed at first glance? Or was it rather the result of forces that had long matured within Europe itself? What were the reasons and why were Portugal and Spain pioneers in the spread of Europeans? How did factors outside Europe affect the character of this expansion? These are the topics this booklet will cover.

Europe and the Broader World

It is not easy to imagine from today's perspective that Europe was once relatively isolated and self-enclosed, with little knowledge of the places beyond its borders, and no known world map today.

But until the discoveries of the 15th and 16th centuries, Europe had been nurtured more by myth and fantasies about the world outside itself than by factual knowledge.

Among the more reliable sources of information in 15th-century Europe were the writings of classical antiquity and the reports of more recent travelers. Ptolemy's Geography, written in the second century AD, circa 1406

It was rediscovered in Christian Europe by being translated from Greek into Latin. Geography contained a compendium of geographic knowledge from the height of the Roman Empire. Although it gave a fairly accurate description of the immediate areas of Asia and Africa, it was an unreliable source for more remote areas; It gave no clue about the existence of America and other formerly unknown parts of the world. One of the most popular and influential of the works of the traveler was that of the Italian Marco Polo. Marco Polo,

In the late 13th century, he had crossed Asia and visited the palace of the Mongol Emperor in China. Polo provided the idea of Asia as a richer continent with advanced and powerful civilizations in the minds of Europeans. It inspired Polo's "Travels", Prince Henry of Portugal, and (along with Ptolemy) Christopher Columbus. But such sources also had their drawbacks. One of Columbus' targets on his western voyage across the Atlantic, the Mongol ruler 'Cathay' (China), had long since perished. Late medieval Europe's deep belief that the ancients did everything right (except religion), hindered a critical approach to their geographical artifacts and a practical spirit of inquiry.

Ptolemy and Polo, although scanty and outdated, provided a more reliable source of information by 1400 than the myths, legends, and false travel tales that shaped Late Medieval Europe's concept of the world. The most widely read, and certainly no less influential than Polo's, was Sir John Mendeville's Travels. In his work, the author consists almost entirely of imaginary stories of strange people (for example, with a dog's head) and of the unconventional of the East.

He was talking about his customs. Beliefs of ships daring to sail into unknown seas far away and falling off the edge of the world or perish in the boiling seas of the "hot zone" also remained in popular fantasies. Such fears were a powerful barrier to investigations and practical research. But there were other fantasies that spoke of the existence of lost islands, of the mighty Christian king Prester John, who ruled somewhere beyond the Muslim regions in Asia or Africa, and the continent of Atlantis in the West. Although these were also unrealistic, they played a certain role in the development of 15th century expeditions.

A similar mix of fantasy and half-truth is to be found in medieval maps. In earlier maps, Jerusalem, as the spiritual center of Christianity, is seen at the center of a circular world with the known continents arranged symmetrically around itself. These mappae mundi (maps of the world) had no use value for sailors and travelers, and were not prepared with such intent. Later maps influenced by Ptolemy show the northern part of Africa and western Asia quite accurately; but how Africa extends south and whether the Indian Ocean is a landlocked sea remains unclear. There was no trace of America, Australia or the Pacific on these maps. Map makers, Europe's Africa and Asia' they compensated for their ignorance of the hinterland by drawing rivers and mountains of their own making; they added fictitious information or made it seem like long-dead monarchs were still in power in these regions.

Europe was not alone in this ignorance and abstraction. In 1400 the world was divided into many different communities or civilizations with little or no relationship to each other. Some communities, such as the peoples of Central and South America, were completely cut off from other continents. Great Asian civilizations such as China and India had wider trade relations. However, these relations were not enough to overcome their basic cultural isolation and economic isolation. To some extent this isolation was due to a series of geographical barriers such as seas, deserts, mountain ranges and dense forests. But this was reinforced by the absence of transport, communication, and control that united disparate peoples and regions into larger divisions. Usually though,

China was a striking example of this. In 1400, China's maritime technology was in many respects equal to that of Europe. Between 1405 and 1433, China had regular trade relations with southeast Asia, with expeditions as far as Sri Lanka and East Africa under Admiral Cheng Ho. Around this time or earlier, Chinese ships sailed to Northern Australia and possibly as far as the Pacific coast of North America. Confucian China considered itself culturally and politically superior to its neighbors and saw them as barbarians who merely paid tribute to the Chinese emperors. It seems that his desire to search for tribute and wealth and items for the Chinese palace was the driving factor in Cheng Ho's travels; Otherwise, about the rest of the world, China.

not enter. In the Chinese Empire, commerce and merchants had a low status, as opposed to the merchant class, which held an extremely important position in Europe. Cheng Ho's expeditions followed suit, and China retreated into its shell just as the Portuguese began to descend off the West African coast and seek a Western route to

India.

Arab and Indian Muslim traders had established a complex and dense trading system in the Indian Ocean. But they were content to limit their activities to areas known to be profitable and safe. Arab sailors had previously traded directly with China, but seldom ventured further east from the Indonesian islands until 1400. In the southwest, they did not go beyond Mozambique and Madagascar. For further journeys the risk of danger increases and the commercial prospects did not seem to be realized. Similarly, Arab sailors and geographers in the Mediterranean believed that after the Moroccan coast, the dark sea of the Atlantic began, where navigable and ships were torn apart.

In certain respects the Europe of 1400 appeared to be a particularly isolated and self-enclosed beleaguered civilization, so it did not seem likely to lead an era of exploration and expansion. A plague epidemic called The Black Death that swept across Europe in 1348-49 ravaged the economy and killed a third or more of the population. 200 for the population of Europe to regain its mid-

14th century level.

It took more than a year. In the 16th century, the demand and need for America's mineral wealth arose for the revival of the European economy. Climate change has also contributed to a feeling of beleaguered Europe. In the relatively warm climate conditions that prevailed between the 8th and 14th centuries, settlement and agriculture advanced further in the north and west. Vikings established colonies in Iceland, Greenland and reached Vinland on the northeastern coast of the American mainland. But colder conditions characterized as the "Little Ice Age" put an end to this expansion. The southward advance of Arctic glaciers cut off the northern route to Vinland, jeopardizing relations with Greenland and Iceland.

In the South, the Mediterranean Sea, once the heart of the Roman Empire, was divided between Christian Europe and its Muslim neighbors. In the West, the Portuguese and Spanish states born in the Iberian peninsula had succeeded in pushing back step by step the Muslims who had conquered the whole region in the 8th century. Until 1400, only Granada (as a true representative of the Castile State) remained in the hands of the Muslims. It was captured in 1492 after a 10-year struggle. But although the Muslim forces were eventually driven from their peninsula, the Portuguese and Castiles faced greater difficulties in carrying their crusade beyond the Strait of Gibraltar and into Muslim North Africa. Portugal built the Moroccan Port of Ceuta in 1415, which most historians regard as the true beginning of the Age of Discovery. you got hold of it. However, attempts to expand this bridgehead position had little success. Portugal in 1437

forces suffered a decisive defeat at Tangier. After the conquest of Granada, the Castilians settled in Melilla in 1497; but their desire to go further in North Africa was thwarted, first by the effectiveness of local Muslim resistance, and later by the expanding power of the Turks.

At the eastern end of the Mediterranean, the Ottoman Turks were on the rise in the 15th and early 16th centuries. Constantinople, the last remaining city of the once mighty empire of Byzantium, was conquered by the Turks in 1453. In 1516-17 the Turks defeated rival rulers of Egypt and Syria, the Mamluks, and extended their control over the southern shores of the Mediterranean. The Turks also advanced into the Balkans; they even threatened Vienna in 1529. Turks of nomadic and equestrian origin from Central Asia took over the maritime legacy of the Byzantines when Constantinople fell and became a major force in Mediterranean waters. In 1571, the Turks settled firmly in the eastern Mediterranean, although they were stopped at the battle of Lepanto (Lepanto) off Greece. Thus, in the WestFor centuries it effectively confined Christian Europe and prevented its natural ways of expanding into the immediate areas of Africa and Asia. The consolidated power of Islam therefore required that any era of European exploration and conquest must first make a dramatic leap beyond the immediate borders of Europe.

Despite periodic wars, Christian Europe has learned a lot from the Islamic world. Both the preservation of Greek science and philosophy and the transmission of scientific and agricultural knowledge and technology to Europe from distant lands such as India and China are the works of the Islamic world. The significance of this Islamic-Asian contribution to the European Age of Discovery will be discussed later in this book. Internally, in the period between 1000 and 1400, there were economic and technological developments in Europe, the effects of which were far reaching. Especially in Northern Europe, farming techniques were developed and these techniques contributed to the growth of agricultural yields. There was an expansion in trade by land and sea. Increasing activities are not only in the Mediterranean, but also in the Baltic Sea and the North Sea. It was also seen between Northern and Southern Europe. With the growth of trade and shipping, great advances were also made in banking and finance, especially in the northern Italian cities of Pisa, Florence, Genoa and Venice. The vitality underlying the European economy and the quest to feed it with more trade and new resources created the main driving force behind European expansionism in the 15th and 16th centuries. However, the formations that created this movement were also shaped by factors that were not purely economic. The vitality underlying the European economy and the quest to feed it with more trade and new resources created the main driving force behind European expansionism in the 15th and 16th centuries. However, the formations that created this movement were also shaped by factors that were not purely economic. The vitality underlying the European economy and the quest to feed it with more trade and new resources created the main driving force behind European expansionism in the 15th and 16th centuries. However, the formations that created this movement were also shaped by factors that were not purely economic. The vitality underlying the European economy and the quest to feed it with more trade and new resources created the main driving force behind European expansionism in the 15th and 16th centuries. However, the formations that created this movement were also shaped by factors that were not purely economic.

Spices and Gold

The West's image of Asia and Africa today, 15th and 16th century. century is very different from the image of the European.   parts of these continents with the phenomena of poverty, famine, disease, and economic backwardness. We call these the Third World or developing countries. We compare the rich "North" (includes Europe and North America) with the poor "South" (includes India, China, and Black Africa). But four or five centuries ago, Europe saw itself in certain respects as the poor neighbor of Asia and Africa. Not only the travellers' reports, but also the products of these regions shaped European impressions of these continents. Gold, various jewellery, silks, tapestries, pictorial murals, spices and porcelain gave rise to an image of abundance, wealth and a creative industry.

Late Medieval Europe was located at the end of two great long-distance trade routes. One is the spice trade connecting Europe to Asia, and the other is the gold trade route connecting Europe to Africa.

Although periodically interrupted by wars, invasions, and the collapse of empires, trade routes have remained open since the time of the Romans, bringing silk, spices, jewelry, and other valuables from China, Indonesia, India, and Persia to Europe via Asia. The importance of the silk trade declined as Europe developed its own products. But Europe had nothing to replace the spice of Asia. The spice is found in Asia on the Indonesian islands - Clove, a type of spice native to Asia, in the Moluccas, nutmeg and mace in the Banda islands, and pepper

it was mostly grown in Sumatra - or Sri Lanka (cinnamon-cinnamon), formerly known as Ceylon, and southwestern India (pepper). In Marco Polo's time, spices were transported from Western Asia to the Black Sea and the Near East countries (Levant) by land and by caravans. With the disintegration of the Mongol Empire, this route became very dangerous, and by 1400 Arab and Indian traders transported the spice by sea to ports on the Red Sea. Spices coming here were transported by land to the Mediterranean ports of Egypt and Syria, and were bought from there by Venetian and Genoese merchants to be distributed and sold in Europe.

Today, spice may not seem like a valuable commodity to us to require such an elaborate and extensive trading system. Pepper is a daily consumption item and is relatively inexpensive. Today we pay little attention to spices of any kind. But in the 15th and 16th centuries, there was a great demand for all types of spices in Europe. It was used to flavor stale or salted meat products during the winter months when there was enough feed to keep only a few animals alive and a few vegetables, fruits and beverages alternative to daily food. It also made great contributions to spices, pastries, beverages and confectionery products. The Crusaders' experience of spicy oriental food may also have encouraged a European taste for more exotic flavors. Spices are often classified as a luxury: Edward Gibbon

Spices were also a very profitable product for the merchants who traded them. Wealth from the spice trade was one of the economic foundations for the rise of Italian city-states, especially Genoa and Venice. Moreover, spice was one of the few items whose long-distance trade was profitable. They were light in weight but heavy in goods (this was an important factor in the cheap and pre-transport era) and were able to withstand long journeys and frequent transfers.

Gold, the other important product

of Europe's long-distance trade, was more than just a luxury item. In addition to its use for decoration and display in churches, palaces, and the homes of the wealthy, it was essential to Europe's money and expanding commercial system. Italian city-states, whose commercial and financial activities were growing, basically converted their circulating currency into gold: Florence and Genoa minted gold from 1252, and Venice from 1284. Even the poorer states of Europe, such as Portugal, were quite willing to base their money on the same prestigious foundation. In addition, Europe needed gold to maintain its domestic economy and to use it for payments in its trade with the East. Europe had few products that were valid on the Asian market: Therefore, he had to buy the spice with precious metals. Silver was mined in Germany and Hungary, but Europe was poor in gold mines. The many mineral deposits that used to extract gold were now exhausted; large quantities of gold were destroyed by plunder and trade with the East. Thus, in Late Medieval Europe, it controlled both internal economic development.There was a "gold scarcity" that created a strong driving force for trade and overseas exploration.

Small but significant amounts of gold came to Europe from West Africa during the late Middle Ages. These golds were obtained through surface mining and liquidation processes in the Bambuk region of the upper Senegal River and Bure in Upper Niger. There was also an efficient production of gold in the Akan region of present-day Ghana (the colonial "Gold Coast") in the late 15th century, partially meeting European demand. From these sources in West Africa, gold was brought by local traders, usually in the form of gold dust, to towns such as Timbuktu on the southern edge of the Sahara. There, the gold bought by Arab and Berber traders is passed through the desert by caravans of camels and then in the ports of North Africa by Genoese, Venetian, It was sold to Catalan and Jewish merchants. Traders crossing the Sahara traded textiles, copper, salt, and other goods in demand south of the desert, in exchange for this West African or "Guinean" gold (the term "Guinean gold" is a relic reminding of the importance this gold resource once had). they sold. Although Europe had no direct contact with this gold-producing area before 1400, information about its location was transmitted quite accurately through Arab and Jewish intermediaries, fueling European greed for money. they sold salt and other goods in demand in the south of the desert. Although Europe had no direct contact with this gold-producing area before 1400, information about its location was transmitted quite accurately through Arab and Jewish intermediaries, fueling European greed for money. they sold salt and other goods in demand in the south of the desert. Although Europe had no direct contact with this gold-producing area before 1400, information about its location was transmitted quite accurately through Arab and Jewish intermediaries, fueling European greed for money.

Gold and spices were not the only commodities that, though most glamorous, lured Europeans to reach beyond their shores in search of trade and wealth. Even grain, a staple, was once imported from Morocco and the Atlantic.

were imported from the islands (Azore, Madeira, and the Canary Islands). In the late 14th and early 15th centuries, these areas were colonized and cultivated by European immigrants. Ğker was even more closely tied to European expansionism. The production and consumption of sugar was learned from the Arabs (another relic of medieval Europe's relationship with the Islamic world). Sugar was first produced on the Mediterranean islands and in suitable regions of Sicily and Spain. But increasing demand has spurred attempts to seek new production areas. It became a pioneer crop in Madeira and the Canary Islands, then on the island of Sao Thome in the Gulf of Guinea in the late 15th century, and then across the Atlantic in Brazil and West India, where it continues to the present day. Fish was also taken to Europe, especially by the Portuguese. It was sought further and further afield off the coast of Northwest Africa and in the North Atlantic, rather than on the near shores of the . Dried and salted cod was an important item in Portugal's trade with the rest of Europe.

On the other hand, a brutal slave trade began. As a result of the expulsion of Muslims from the Iberian peninsula and the effects of the Black Death, southern Portugal, in particular, faced a major problem of underpopulation. The black slave trade long accompanied gold caravan expeditions across the Sahara to North Africa. The slave trade was expanding to meet the needs of southern Europe. During thc voyage of early expeditions down the West African coast, the Portuguese sought to work as laborers on Portuguese mansions, and later as the workforce of the expanding sugar economy in the Atlantic islands.

They bought or captured slaves to meet their needs. The joint European movement for expansionism, overseas exploitation of sugar and slaves was a savage feature of the 17th and 18th centuries, and thus began even before Columbus crossed the Atlantic in 1492.

Therefore, the economic drive behind expansionism was not market-seeking concern for European goods. In the 15th and 16th centuries, Europeans faced great difficulties in trying to sell textiles and other products in Africa and Asia. Europe's age of industrialization and the mass production of machine-made products still stood as a distant and future development. European overseas surveys were for trade and the resources that formed part of the European trading system. But expansionism, the result of commercial capitalism developing in Europe, confronts us with a clear contradiction: if economic motives were of such fundamental importance, Italy, the most economically advanced region of Europe, Why did it seem to fail to play an important role in the overseas expansion of this period? Why, instead, were the economically more backward Portugal and Castile the pioneering researcher and the first European states to seek to establish their overseas empires? The answer to these questions is complex and involves a number of factors. But above all it should be noted that Italy made a very important contribution to the Age of Discovery.

Italy

Partly because of the uncertainty of national identities and borders in the 15th and 16th centuries, soldiers and sailors, as well as European explorers, scholars, merchants, could move from the service of one country to the service of another country relatively freely. This mobility, along with the newly discovered printing press, played an important role in the dissemination of information about the first expeditions throughout Europe (especially despite some Portuguese attempts to protect the secrecy of their findings). The Portuguese, indeed, as the first travelers, lost the most by providing information and personnel to other countries. By contrast, Castile owed its rapid and dramatic entry into the field of research in the late 15th and early 16th centuries to the famous Portuguese Magellan and Italian Columbus, who were not affiliated with a group.

Christopher Columbus is a prime example of the importance of mobility among early explorers and Italy's contribution to the Age of Discovery. Columbus was born in Genoa about 1451, later settling in Portugal, married to a Portuguese woman, and first presented to the Portuguese court his project of traveling west to China. Here he was rejected and sought French and British support before finally finding state patronage provided by Isabella, queen of Castile. John Cabot's career is very similar to that of Columbus. He was also a native of Genoa. Like Columbus, Cabot was interested in his plans for searches in the western ocean.

King of England VII, following the news of Columbus's return, to find a government to show He struggled in vain until Henri promised to support an expedition in 1496. Unlike a unified Chinese empire, Europe consisted of a series of states with varying interests and aspirations. Therefore, for adventurers and idealists, there was a possibility of realizing their projects if they managed to secure patronage in their own country or in another receiving country. On the other hand, at the beginning of the travels, state or royal support was mandatory. The costs and risks of procuring and equipping ships for major voyages far exceeded the strength of a solo trader or adventurer. In addition, using the ports and ships of the seafarers, employing their sailors,

In response to the patronage of Portugal, Spain, and England, the Italians also put at the disposal of Western Europe their ideas and mastery of particular maritime techniques, particularly in map-making and in the

Mediterranean. To a certain extent they also brought the science of the Italian Renaissance, especially information in the more recently rediscovered classical works such as Ptolemy's Geography.

There is some debate about the origin of the name "America" used for the western continent. That name is the one who was the customs collector in Bristol and paid Cabot's official salary.

It is claimed to come from Richard Ameryk. But there is an older and perhaps more accurate view that the name America derives from the Florentine businessman Amerigo Vespucci, whose letters, published and widely circulated in the sixteenth century, helped promote the idea of a new continent in Europe. If this view is correct, it is a fitting tribute to the role played by the Italians in the discovery of the "New World" and the dissemination of knowledge about it.

The contribution of the Italians was also of an economic nature. With the development of trade in the late Middle

Ages, traders from Genoa and other Italian city-states established trading colonies in the western Mediterranean and Portugal. Much of the trade with North Africa was conducted through them, and Madeira's sugar production and exports owed its existence largely to the Genoese finances. Formerly a major commercial area of the Genoese, the Black Sea lost its importance as a gateway for trade with distant parts of Asia, and was already in the hands of the Turks in the 15th century. Thereupon, the Genoese turned their attention to the Western Mediterranean. Genoa merchants and financiers generally maintained close relations with Portugal and Castile, despite some initial friction. Francisco Pinelo, a wealthy Genoese financier, had helped with the high cost of Columbus' first and second voyages across the Atlantic. In return for this attitude, he was rewarded in 1503, by being appointed to the Casa de Contratacion (Chamber of Commerce) in Seville, which oversaw commercial relations between Spain and the New World. Genoese, Florentine and German capitalists

they also helped finance the first

Portuguese voyages to the Indies: in 1505, the Florentines and Genoans allocated 30,000 florins for the large Portuguese fleet leaving that year for the East. On the return, the Genoans made huge profits on their capital investment and played a large part in the sale of spices, sugar and silver that flowed overseas to Seville and Lisbon.

For this reason, the Italians were largely content to participate indirectly in the Age of Discovery. There were other reasons why the Italians did not attempt to take a more direct role. Italian galleys and merchant ships were better suited to the calm waters of the Mediterranean than the rough seas and vast expanses of the Atlantic. A Genoese galley, which sailed in 1291 to find a sea route to the Indies, was never heard from again. After this event, the Italians relied on the more suitable ships and naval prowess of the Portuguese and Castiles for their Atlantic trade and voyages.

Its geographical location, which made Italy the center of Mediterranean trade and placed it at the crossroads of trade routes from Africa and Asia, was at a disadvantage in an age of exploration of the Atlantic. Long-established commercial traditions, especially among the Venetians, fostered commercial conservatism and a reluctance to adapt to new conditions. Accustomed to turning to the East for centuries for their trade and wealth, the Venetians sailed a long series of seas between 1499 and 1573.

With their wars, they resisted the expansion of Turkish power in the Eastern Mediterranean. But the Venetians were not inclined to wage a religious war against Islam. They had traded with the Moslem Mamluks of Egypt and Syria in the past and sought ways to negotiate with the Turks in order to re-start the valuable spice trade. In this they partially succeeded, for example, by making a temporary treaty with the Turks in 1519. It was once thought that the opening of Portuguese roads to the spice regions had a rapid and sustained devastating effect on the Venetian economy. It is now clear that this is not so. By about 1520, the long-distance spice trade by land was revived, and Venice was again a major importer and distributor of spices. Portugal' The merchants had high commercial prices, and the quality of their spice was said to have deteriorated from long sea voyages and was inferior to that of the Venetians. The partial recovery allayed Venetians' anxieties and discouraged Venetian merchants from any thought of making any fundamental changes to traditional trading patterns. The city of Venice's long-term decline; To the Portuguese and later to the Dutch! owes much to his general neglect of the burgeoning Atlantic trade, as well as to the spice trade. The city of Venice's long-term decline; To the Portuguese and later to the Dutch! owes much to his general neglect of the burgeoning Atlantic trade, as well as to the spice trade. The city of Venice's long-term decline; To the Portuguese and later to the Dutch! owes much to his general neglect of the burgeoning Atlantic trade, as well as to the spice trade.

On the other hand, certain political and cultural factors prevented Italy from participating in the Age of Discovery on a larger scale. The palaces and city-states of Renaissance Italy competed to reveal their wealth and artistic achievements. The country's ostentatious spending and growth within Italy mean less resources are available for expansionist projects on distant continents.

led to it. In contrast to the poorer but correspondingly more daring Atlantic coast states, they developed a behavior of looking inward and self-satisfied. His first Atlantic voyages also coincided with a period of armed conflict with an invasion in Italy. Divided from within, Italy was unprepared to resist French and Spanish ambitions on the peninsula, and its economy was plagued by the effects of war. By contrast, the Western European states were emerging as more unified and powerful political entities that provided a sufficiently stable and secure environment in their countries to gain overseas exploration and expansion experiments.

Portugal and Spain

Perched on the southwestern edge of Christian Europe, Portugal was one of Europe's first national states to stabilize its political borders. Before the end of the 13th century, the Algarve, the last Muslim region to the south, had been conquered, and by 1580 Portugal had successfully resisted attempts to annex itself into a larger Iberian state. Intermittent conflicts with Castile turned into open warfare in 1383-1411 and 1474-79, serving both to strengthen Portugal's sense of different identity and to intensify rivalry between the two states in North Africa and the Atlantic islands. The Treaty of Alcaçovas, which ended the Wars of Succession in 1479, also included the Atlantic islands, Azores and Madeira. He divided the territory between Portugal, which held it but had to recognize the demands of the Castiles for the Canary Islands, and its rival. Ceuta (North

A port in Morocco) was captured by the Portuguese in 1415, causing concern in Castile, especially since it was the port lining the Spanish side of the Strait of Gibraltar. But Castile did not see Portugal's entry into the interior of the North African mainland until the fall of Granada in 1492.

For a poor and small country like Portugal, which was unlikely to expand its territory at the expense of its European neighbors, overseas expansion was of great political and economic importance. The majority of the Portuguese population consisted of peasants, numbering about one million at the end of the 15th century, and the country was too poor and rocky to afford anything more than a medium agricultural economy. Portugal lacked in commercial expertise and the resources needed to participate in established Mediterranean trade. But in addition to exporting its own olive oil and wine, it was well positioned to engage in the expanding trade between Northern and Southern Europe, bringing grain, wine, and sugar from the Azores and Madeira, and searching for cod and tuna in the Atlantic. Its position in the Atlantic could thus turn into a commercial advantage. Atlantic' The tide of winds and currents on the outskirts made Portugal (along with the adjacent Spanish coast) an ideal departure and return point for ships trading with the islands and dredging the ocean for fishing. The commercial and maritime orientation of the Portuguese expansion thus took place at an early stage and contrasted with the predominant continental character of the Castilian expansion.Portugal's domestic political and social conditions also supported expansionism. The Avis dynasty, which came to power with the 1383-85 revolution,

It generally suited the aspirations of Portugal's small but thriving commercial middle class and saw the economic benefits to be derived from the Portuguese's growing overseas power. Famous for his expeditions to explore the West African coasts, Prince Henry the Seafarer was also advancing Portuguese colonial activities in the Atlantic islands and developing sugar production in these islands. The Portuguese nobility was right to share this desire for expansion. As wars of conquest had become almost impossible in their own regions, they looked first to Africa and then to Asia for an opportunity to add land, wealth and valuable goods to their country.

Contrary to all this, Spain was more traditional, looking more towards the Mediterranean than the Atlantic. Eastern Spanish Aragonians and Catalans had previously directed their commercial and political ambitions towards Italy, the Balearic Islands and North Africa. The process of unification and national cohesion was also behind Portugal. Although the marriage of Ferdinand of Aragon and Isabella of Castile in 1469 and the victory in a series of wars in 1474-79 led to the unification of the two kingdoms, both states preferred to remain separate, keeping their own laws and institutions in place. But even this level of unification freed Christian Spain from the internal divisions that had preoccupied it so much and gave it energy and strength to turn its attention to expansionist policies. Isabella's 1492' of Columbus

Like Portugal, Spain was deeply affected by the Reconquista (the centuries-old struggle to retake the peninsula from Muslim Moroccans). The tradition of the Crusades had a strong influence on the thinking and behavior of the Castilians. With the defeat of Granada, Isabella's active power policy of expelling the Jews, forcible conversion of the Muslims and establishing the Inquisition is a testament to her determination to uproot the non-Christian powers that formed part of Medieval Spain. With only a narrow strait separating Christian Spain from Muslim North Africa and growing Turkish influence in the Mediterranean, Isabella's overseas expansionism was a continued struggle against Islam and, when Columbus returned, he converted to Christianity.

Religious motives were not isolated from other factors. It reinforced other factors and was often used to justify economic and political goals. In the 15th century, religion was inseparable from political or commercial considerations and was part of everyday life. But the importance of religious factors, Portugal and It gave additional confidence and determination to Castile's expansionism. The rigidity of their religious convictions, their deep belief that they had been divinely missioned to overthrow Islam and convert the heathen to the faith, led the Portuguese and Castiles on overseas adventures. Whereas, the more cautious and pragmatic states of Europe, especially Italy, were not going to achieve successful results despite their crazy ideas. Religion is therefore an important factor in explaining the pioneers of the Iberian states in overseas expansion.

The Reconquista had other consequences for Castilian expansionism. As the Muslims were defeated and the borders of Islam were withdrawn, the newly liberated territories joined the Christian Spanish states. Christian colonies were established, new cities were born. This process of assimilation, through conquest and colonization, was repeatedly repeated in overseas areas such as the Canary Islands and the Americas. The continental character of this expansion was associated with the commercial empires of Genoa and Venice, with a few strategically or commercially important islands in the Mediterranean, such as Rhodes and Crete, as well as small colonies in commercial areas within the territory of other states, such as Lisbon, Seville, or Alexandria. it was contradictory. Portugal's empire born from the sea, Castile's New World

Contrary to the Spanish aristocracy and the weak Portuguese aristocracy, the fact that Christian wars and conquests were in the border region, through military adventures, wealth, land and prestige.

and a sense of contempt for trade. This attitude resulted in a large part of Castile's trade falling into the hands of foreigners, especially Genoans. A sense of contempt for handicraft as well as trade existed even among the poorer Castilians. Francisco Pizarro, himself a peasant, said when he conquered Peru in 1533: "I came here to get gold, not to plow like a peasant." Within Spain itself, the spirit of a dynamic and turbulent border region was vividly preserved by one of Europe's most extensive rural economies. The itinerant sheep herders of Estremadura in western Spain and the cattle breeders of Andalusia in the south, the Spanish Conquistador (conqueror) in the Americas, with their many hardy soldiers and immigrants. formed the basis of their Thus, paradoxically, the relative economic backwardness of Portugal and Spain and the existence of the tradition of crusades in the Iberian border region, together with its geographical location, explain why this region led overseas expansion over other European states.

Technology and Research

The Age of Discovery did not cut Europe openly and directly from its past. Many of the motives that drove the development of this era, such as Prince Henry's search for Prester John, Isabella's crusade against the Muslims, and Columbus' attempts to reach China and Japan as described in Marco Polo's Travels, continued to reflect the medieval mentality. Even when new lands are reached, the first reaction of Europeans is these new phenomena,

was to try to reconcile the classical books with the relevant information found in the Bible and medieval texts. Even Columbus, until his death in 1506, thought he had discovered the islands off the Asian mainland and not a New World hitherto unknown to Europe. America's early explorers envisioned themselves as having been transported to biblical paradise and encountering the people and places described in classical mythologies or medieval romances. Reason and empirical observation only gradually came to dominate myth, fantasy, and fear. However, 15th- and 16th-century Europeans, besides the legacy of the past, adapted and perfected existing maritime technology and geography,

The Portuguese studies of West Africa, led by Prince Henry, are a striking example of the process of experimentation and learning. To the south of the Canary Islands, as far as Cape Bojadar, ships sailed in familiar waters: they sailed close to the African coast and could always find winds and currents to take them home. But the gusts of wind near the coast and the choppy waters of the promontory seemed to confirm the sailors' fears of "an ocean of monsters and a boiling sea that could not be navigable and shattered the ship's rails" beyond. Passing through Cape Bojadar in 1434 and sailing further in the Atlantic and finding a way back to Portugal, Prince Henry's sailors thus crossed not only the physical limits of medieval seafaring, but also psychologically they have provided adevelopmentand the whole of the world

They paved the way for the exploration of the oceans.

Europeans of the 15th and 16th centuries used two maritime traditions, one originating from the East and the other coming from European voyage experiments in their own waters, to exploit in their voyages. Although it is difficult to pinpoint the transition process, a number of important helpers are known to be of Asian origin. The value of the moving magnetic needle used to determine the north direction was probably first understood by the Chinese and then spread to Europe by Indian and

Arab sailors. Europeans may also have learned to use the astrolabe, an instrument that made it possible to determine a ship's position from the angle the sun and stars make with the observer, by contacting Arab sailors in the Mediterranean. which Christian Europe has acquired, The characteristic latin sail or triangular sail of Muslim boats may also have passed from the Arabs. But the Europeans in any case adapted and perfected the naval traditions and instruments they had acquired from the East. For example, the magnetic pointer was fixed with a brass needle on a card showing the main points of the compass. This developed device proved reliable enough as the main naval instrument used by ships far from land in the Mediterranean until the early 15th century. Similarly, the slightly modified latin sail came to be used not as an alternative to the square sails of European ships, but as an additional motive device alongside them. Dealing with rough seas, winds, currents and large areas of the Atlantic,

required. However, as soon as the Portuguese turned the Cape of Good Hope and entered the Indian Ocean, they made rapid development through Asian shipping. This development was largely fueled by the knowledge and ingenuity of Asian guides and sailors. In 1498, Vasco da Gama owed his direct sailing from the East African port of Malindi to Calicut on the southwest coast of India to the aid of a Muslim Indian who knew the monsoon winds of the West Indian Ocean. Monsoon winds directly determined trade between India and East Africa, blowing from the southwest to the northeast from April to August and vice versa from December to March. Therefore, it took about eighty years for the Portuguese to open the Atlantic sea route from Morocco to the Cape of Good Hope.

The adoption of maritime aids and instruments of Oriental origin, and the use of the technical ingenuity of Indian ocean guides, indicate that the Age of Discovery had a scope that could be seen as a European-Asian achievement rather than a purely European one. But Europe's ability to adapt and expand knowledge and technology from outside sources and to combine them with its own maritime experiments has given it a decisive advantage over Asian shipping.

The spread of maritime trade and shipping, especially in northern and western European waters, during the Late Middle Ages, improved maritime transport, as did the Portuguese expeditions of Atlantic travel in the 15th century. He whipped up his techniques and shipbuilding. The development of a ship's rudder has allowed for more confident steering of boats, especially in the strong tides of north coast waters. Guidance action in the North Sea and the Baltic was supported by the preparation of plans that included all the accumulated information about winds, tides, shallows, and coastal features, and showing the ships' headings. The Mediterranean equivalent of these written guides formed the basis for nautical charts known as portalans describing coastal features, ports, and marine hazards. As nautical charts, portalans were still in a relatively primitive stage in the 15th century: for example, they treated the sea as a flat surface, not taking into account the tilt of the ground.The diagrams and portalans were very useful for guidance in Europe's widely circulated coastal waters or for short trips away from land, but the Atlantic was not mapped, so they were not used in unknown waters. There, rather than guidance, the ability to determine a ship's position and steer it in one direction without reference to a known landmark was essential. A rational approach and experience in solving problems was vital in acquiring this ability. Portuguese sailors; Until the middle of the 15th century, when they went beyond Cape Bojador and traveled northwestward in a great loop (or volta) away from the African coast, they found themselves back in Portugal.

They had learned that they would find the westerly winds to carry them. Their familiarity with the North Atlantic voltaic helped the Portuguese as they crossed the Equator and began their attempt to turn around southern Africa. In time they realized that the Atlantic westerly wind was the northern reflection of the South Atlantic wind system, so that to cross the Cape of Good Hope it was necessary to first turn the ships southwest and then find the westerly winds that would carry them eastward into the Indian Ocean. This maneuver was first developed by Bartholomew Dias in 1486 (or perhaps on his hitherto forgotten later voyages) and used by Vasco da Gama in 1497 to navigate safely to the Indian Ocean around South Africa. South Atlantic' With such a sweeping sweep in the middle of the middle of nowhere, the Portuguese passed close to South America. They may have seen South America before 1492, when Columbus reached the West Indies. In 1500, Pedro Cabral followed the south voltae on the road to India and landed on the Brazilian coast. (Cabral thus initiated the Portuguese claim on South American territories.) Columbus also benefited from the knowledge accumulated during the 15th century about Atlantic winds and currents. In 1492 he crossed the ocean from east to west following the trade winds, and then turned early the next year, turning north against the trade winds until he found westerly winds to take him back to Europe the following year. The uncharted Atlantic Frequent long distance travels from land in the past forced the Portuguese to rely more heavily on nautical devices such as the compass, astrolabe, and quadrant. The difficulty of determining a ship's position in the Atlantic

In 1484, he prompted the Portuguese king John II to set up a commission of mathematicians to find the best method of determining latitude by observing the sun. Existing declination tables giving the sun angles above the horizon at different locations have been reviewed and simplified for use in navigation. A mathematician was then sent on a trip to the West African coast to check the accuracy of these tables with practical observations. Thus, research and marine technology were developed together. In fact, long-distance voyages, encouraged by the development of better ships and naval equipment, presented Europeans with practical problems that they attempted to solve through reason and experience. Undoubtedly, there were many errors and omissions. It was not until the 18th century, for example, that a satisfactory device for determining longitude was developed. Many of the sailors and sailors of the time used the presence of birds or floating plants, the color of the sea, the character of cloud formations, etc., to determine proximity to land. continued to rely on traditional signs such as By 1600, however, great advances were seen in the development of European shipping.

One of the most important factors behind 15th and 16th century sea voyages was the advances in ship design and construction. Much of the Mediterranean trade in the Middle Ages was carried out by heavy, wide, round-bottomed boats propelled by one or more latin sails. Flat and narrow-bottomed, propelled by a set of oars, galleys could reach significant speeds in short periods of time. However, these are not bulky goods such as cereals, they are light and flavored such as spices.

It was more suitable for the transport of valuable cargo and naval warfare. In addition, although in the 14th and 15th centuries large Venetian galleys made annual voyages to Flanders (the medieval country consisting of today's Belgium and its neighboring parts of France and the Netherlands) and England, the galleys generally survived the harsh conditions of the Atlantic. was not suitable. Northern European shipbuilders built powerful boats known as kogs (cogs), in contrast to Mediterranean ships. Built for trade in the

Baltic and North Seas, these boats sailed with a single square sail, and were built by overlapping pieces of pavement, unlike Mediterranean boats, which were neatly tied and the seams at the bottom were waterproofed with filler. The advantage of cogs,

Distinctions and distinct identity differences between northern and southern ships persisted into the 15th century. But with the development of trade between the two regions, hybrid boats combining characteristics of both styles began to appear along the coasts of Portugal and Southern Spain. The most famous of these new types of ships was the caravel. It was a small ship. It would rarely weigh more than 70 tons and be longer than 20 m. It had a straight keel and a rudder at the stern, propelled by two or three lattice sails or, as in later periods, a combination of latin and square sails. Such boats were probably first developed for local trade around the Portuguese and Spanish coasts. But in about 1440, Prince Henry adopted them for African research. below her deck

Although there were few rooms for crew and cargo, the shallow draft made the caravel ideal for research near shore and in bays. Latin sails allowed her to be driven with light wind, sailing downwind or navigating. The caravel could also be fast. With a favorable wind, he crossed the entire Atlantic from the Cape Verde Islands to the Antilles in 21 days. This speed was not exceeded until the advent of steamships in the 19th century. Two of the three ships Columbus sailed in 1492, the Pinta and the Nina, were caravels. The third was the flagship Santa Maria. The slower, square-sailing Santa Maria proved less suitable for research. It became unusable after hitting a coral reef in the Indies.

Caravels, ideal for research, were less suitable for undertaking longer journeys and carrying cargo as new trade routes opened. For this reason, they were rarely used in Portugal's eastern trade. In their place, ships of very large build, called carrack or naos, with high fronts, wide beams and three or four decks began to be used. The tonnage of these ships increased from about 400 tons at the beginning of the 16th century to about 1000 tons 50 years later and to 2000 tons in the 17th century. A mizzen (mizzen) latin sail was retained on the carracks, but was combined with several square sails to achieve a larger sail width. the end of the 16th century andAt the turn of the century, the Dutch and English began to surpass the Portuguese and the Spanish in the design of war and merchant ships with special characteristics.

In the 15th and 16th centuries, Europe was able to take advantage of its position at the edge of a medieval world, spreading from the Atlantic to the China Sea by improving its ships and naval technology. The once intimidating "ship-shattering sea of darkness" became Europe's main highway, allowing it to trade directly with Africa and Asia, and to harvest America's natural resources and mineral wealth for its own use. A Europe that could not establish dominance on the seas would be isolated and largely dependent on its own resources. Against a resisting and resilient Islam, the latest expansionist movements in Christian Europe could have resulted in an earlier exhaustion in the Holy Land (Palestine) or North Africa. In an age when land transport had become slow and dangerous, Caravels and Caravels created unforeseen opportunities for exploration, trade and conquest for Europeans across all the world's oceans. Europeans were also quick to seize this opportunity.

Africa

The importance of Africa in 15th and 16th century European expansionism is often overlooked. It is too easily seen as a trivial beginning for Portugal to discover a direct sea route to the East and the first crossing to the west across the Atlantic. In fact, these voyages, financed by Henry the Sailor between 1419 and his death in 1460, had the purpose of exploring the African coast and exploiting African resources. The possibility of carving a new route to the spice islands of the East may have been conceived by Henry only in the last years of his life. This idea was not immediately grasped as a practical goal until the reigns of John II (1481-95) and Manuel (1495-1521).

One of Prince Henry's main aims in arranging expeditions to the south was to oust the Muslim traders of North Africa and establish direct contact with the gold-producing region known to extend beyond the Sahara. For the first two decades, Henry's ships spoke of a barren coast as they returned, with a very sparse population and little commercial potential. But when an expeditionary group reached the mouth of the Senegal River in 1444-45, the Portuguese witnessed a more fertile and populous region and the availability of gold.

However, the Portuguese found it impossible to penetrate the inland gold fields. densely populated area that separates the coast from gold-producing areas and African, local people

rainforests made it impossible for the Portuguese to advance inland. The Portuguese had fewer advantages on land than they had at sea. Other than the Gambia, there were no large rivers suitable for the passage of ships that would allow them to go inland. Despite a primitive and rather insecure nature, their firearms were often less effective than African spears or bows and arrows. While the African rulers gathered thousands of warriors, the Portuguese, whose resources and manpower were weak in their country, could gather very few people. Tropical diseases such as malaria and yellow fever killed many soldiers and sailors. They therefore had to stay on the coast and rely on African intermediaries who brought them gold in exchange for European and North African goods such as textiles and copper, or necklaces and slaves, as on the Guinean coast. In this way, the Portuguese were able to partially turn the former Saharan gold trade to the coast. In the late 15th and early 16th centuries, West Africa delivered about 400 kg per year to the Portuguese. provided gold. In order to protect this trade from European rivals as well as African rulers (for trade was largely dependent on their goodwill and personal interests), the Portuguese built a series of forts on the coast. Arguin was built in 1445, then Elmina (the principal outlet for gold from the Akan forest) in 1482, and Axim in 1503. These fortified commercial centers

At the beginning of the 16th century, the Portuguese in south-east Africa, a second gold trade that they did not realize before

they discovered. This trade extended from what is now Zimbabwe to the coastal cities of Sofala and Kilwa. The Portuguese succeeded in taking control of the gold trade to a certain extent by shelling these cities, partially destroying them, and establishing their own bases on the island of Mozambique. They also went inland for several hundred kilometers along the Zambezi valley. However, they failed to establish control over the main gold producing region, as in West Africa.

In addition to gold, the Portuguese initially traded in other African products such as ivory and West African peppers. But when they got used to the Indies and saw that it was a much richer and more lucrative trade area, their interest in these products waned. East Africa remained important to the Portuguese as a gold-supplier to Asian trade and the protector of the western flank in their rule over the Indian Ocean. The only other trade in western Africa in which the Portuguese continued to be interested was the slave trade. Initially, slaves were obtained as a result of attacks carried out along the coast. But by the 1480s the slave trade was now part of Portugal's trade with African states and merchants. During the 15th century, large numbers of slaves were moved to Lisbon for sale: Between 1450 and 51500, an estimated 150,000 slaves were brought to Europe. With the opening of the Americas and especially with the establishment of sugar plantations in Portuguese Brazil in the late 16th century, the slave trade changed direction and grew in volume.

The profitability of the slave trade, combined with the lure of Guinean gold, drew other Europeans to the West African coast. England's involvement in the transatlantic slave trade began in 1562 with Sir John Hawkins. But the most serious threat to Portugal's position on the coast came from the Netherlands in the 1590s. In the 1630s, the Netherlands captured several Portuguese trading ports on the West African coast: Portugal recaptured Angola's slave trading ports of Luanda and Benguela, but forever lost Axim and Elmina on the Gulf of Guinea.

Trade, while essential, was not the only form of Portuguese contact in Africa, hostility to Islam was a constant feature of Portuguese relations with Northwest and East Africa, and the destruction of the mainly Muslim cities of Sofala and Kilwa, the Portuguese commercial passions He owed something to his religious enmity as well. As early as 1494, a group of

Portuguese tasked with searching for Prester John arrived in the modal Christian kingdom of Ethiopia. But further relations developed very slowly. 400 Portuguese soldiers were sent to help the Ethiopians resist a Muslim invasion in 1541-43. But the close alliance that Prince Henry had once dreamed of still didn't stand a chance. Ethiopia, was weaker than that depicted by medieval European fantasy. The Portuguese and Ethiopians had little in common: even the forms of Christianity were very

to Christianize and Europeanize them. One of the most famous of these efforts is the Congo stretching south of the Congo River.

His efforts in the Kingdom. Missionaries, teachers, and artisans were sent from Portugal in the 14990's, and in 1506 a convert (converted) Christian ascended the Congo throne as Alfonso I. This King favored establishing close ties with Portugal, but with the start of Indies trade, Portuguese interest in the region quickly waned. A creative and peaceful relationship was thus lost, and the Kingdom of Congo was handed over to the slave traders. Portugal's economic interests in Africa prevailed to the detriment of its religious idealism.

Asia

Portugal's success in Asia seemed brilliant, at least at first glance. Less than 50 years after Vasco da Gama's arrival at Calicut in southwestern India in 1498, Portuguese naval power had spread across the Indian Ocean from Mozambique in East Africa to Malacca on the Malaya Peninsula. They stretched from Hormuz in the Arabian Gulf to Macau off the South China coast. For most historians, the arrival of the Portuguese symbolized Asia's definitive break with its past. The Indian historian KMPanikkar spoke of an "age of Vasco da Gama" that began in 1498 and ended with the collapse of European Empires in Asia after the Second World War. Other historians who make evaluations from a European point of view, Although their reasons were different, they emphasized that the Portuguese had established themselves in Asia with apparent ease. Some valued the effectiveness of the Portuguese ships and artillery. GB Sansom, on the other hand, describes the success of the Portuguese as their "achievement".

He based it on the fact that their "steadfast spirit" was stronger than the Asian people's will to resist.

We have seen the limitations of the Portuguese power in Africa, despite their naval advantage. What really happened that the Portuguese had such a sudden and dramatic impact on Asia? In the words of JH Plumb, "Is the East at the mercy of Europe?"
Nowhere in Asia did the Portuguese establish a land empire for themselves as the Spanish did in the Americas. Most likely, no such request was ever made. Their main interest was in creating and maintaining a lucrative naval empire. They had neither adequate human and weapon resources nor the incentive to try to seize and hold large territories. Instead, pursuing commercial goals, the Portuguese took advantage of the competitive advantage of local powers to form alliances with monarchs who either prepared to trade with them or fought for them. In Calicut, when the Zamorin (the raja of Cachin. In 1510, further north of Goa, the Portuguese succeeded in forging a credible commercial and military alliance with the Hindu rulers of southern India's Vijayanagar Empire. Like Africa, Asia failed to counter the Portuguese intruders, both commercially and militarily. Such alliances served to protect

Portuguese coastal interests and extend their influence inlant, but

. There was no serious opposition to the Portuguese in these waters until the Dutch and British entered the Indian Ocean about a century later. Despite the presence of opposing forces - the Chinese had defeated the Portuguese at sea in 1521 and 1522 - the ships and firearms of the Portuguese ultimately made them rulers of the Asian seas.

shows that. This struggle initially took the form of open opposition. But later, when the Portuguese ships and heavy artillery showed their strength, the Asians often chose to escape Portuguese control. The lack of interest in naval power and maritime trade by many of Asia's largest states helped the Portuguese to dominate the sea. The Chinese empire of the Ming dynasty, the state of Vijayanagar in southern India, and the Mongol empire founded in northern India in 1526, all of these states considered themselves mainly land empires, deriving their wealth from land and inland trade rather than maritime trade. The rulers of the Vijayanagar state valued trade with the Portuguese, especially the horses they brought from Hormuz.

As in Africa, the initial aggression of the Portuguese was partly due to their religious beliefs. It was religiously unacceptable for them to engage in peaceful trade with the Muslims, even if it was commercially feasible. The spirit of intolerance of the Reconquista had moved from the Iberian peninsula to the Indian Ocean. However, although the Portuguese initially showed serious aggression towards Muslim traders and the rulers they encountered in the East, they made only feeble attempts at the triumph of Christianity in Asia. The arrival of the Jesuits in Goa in 1540 brought a more determined religious spirit to the relations of the Portuguese with Hindus as well as Muslims in India.

brought. But apart from their own small colony and a few successes in South India, such as the conversion of Parava fishermen in 1537, the Portuguese came to realize that they had to be practically tolerant of the established religions of Asia, even Islam, for their commercial interests. Apart from their religious struggles, the Portuguese had to use force to establish themselves in the Asian maritime. Because it was not possible for them to achieve their commercial goals otherwise. Trade in the Indian Ocean was a complex relationship of regional exchanges. Different areas produced different goods. For example, Indian textiles were an important item of trade with East Africa, where they were exchanged for gold and ivory. Gold and ivory were also taken to the Indonesian islands to be exchanged for spices. As Vasco da Gama discovered while trying to buy spices in Calicut in 1498, the Portuguese had no valuable trading commodities to contribute to this trading system, other than copper from Europe and gold from Africa. The anger of the Muslims at the arrival of Christian merchants in a region they had conquered added to the difficulties of the Portuguese in establishing themselves commercially. Therefore, it seemed imperative to use force to enter the trading world of Asia. They had no valuable trade goods to contribute to this trading system, except for copper from Africa and gold from Africa. The anger of the Muslims at the arrival of Christian merchants in a region they had conquered added to the difficulties of the Portuguese in establishing themselves commercially. Therefore, it seemed imperative to use force to enter the trading world of Asia. They had no valuable trade goods to contribute to this trading system, except for copper from Africa and gold from Africa. The anger of the Muslims at the arrival of Christian merchants in a region they had conquered added to the difficulties of the Portuguese in establishing themselves commercially. Therefore, it seemed imperative to use force to enter the trading world of Asia.

He developed a dual system of maritime and commercial control under Afonso de Albuquerque, who was regarded as the true architect of Portuguese rule in the East and was Governor-General of Portuguese India from 1509-1515. The first part of this system is to dominate the most valuable trade routes.

Of the few strategically or commercially important cities for him, it was to capture and hold those that could be captured even with Portugal's limited resources. Captured in 1510, Goa became the center of Portugal's trade with West India and the capital of its administrative activities in the East. In the West, in addition to Mozambique and Mombasa on the East African coast, in 1515 the Portuguese captured Hormuz, an island dominating the entrance to the Arabian Gulf. However, they were unsuccessful in capturing Aden, which would bring them dominion of the Red Sea in 1513 and 1548. Attempts to use their navies to thwart Muslim trade in the Red Sea brought little more than limited success. In the East, Malacca was captured in 1511. Malacca, It was the main gathering point for spice from the Indonesian islands and the meeting place of the Indian Ocean and Chinese trade. Further east, the Portuguese captured several spice-producing islands. Among them was the Moluccas, the main source of various kinds of spices (nutmeg, mace, and cloves). The Portuguese also entered the trading system of the China Sea, establishing bases in Macau for trade with China in 1557 and Nagasaki in Japan.

The second part of the Portuguese attempts to control trade was an introduction to a transit system (cartazes). Accordingly, port officials, who were issued by the Portuguese, were giving passage to Asian boats to carry the goods deemed suitable along special roads. This measure was a greater limitation on Muslim trade activities and freedom of movement in the Indian Ocean. But in fact, the Portuguese monopoly on some valuable products, especially pepper, and other trades.

It was designed to secure the possibility of taxation of Asian shipping. The transit system was also intended to strengthen Portuguese dominance over Asian shipping.Strengthening themselves in this way, the Portuguese increased the profitability of their commercial empire. From the beginning, they were deeply involved in shipping the Asian trade, as well as maintaining the spice trade to Europe, which was their main destination in the East. This sector proved highly profitable for Portuguese traders and civil servants, especially in the East. Portuguese ships, for example, continued a substantial trade of gold, silver, and silk from China to Japan via Macau and Nagasaki. By participating in Asian shipping, the Portuguese adapted to the pre-existing trade model and were only partially successful in forcing a characteristic European trading system into Asian shipping. In commerce as in religion, the influence of the Portuguese was significant, but limited.

The Portuguese empire in the East had a fundamental weakness that made it vulnerable to both internal disruption and external aggression. The number of bases planned by Albuquerque in the early 16th century steadily increased during new attempts to open new trading areas or fill gaps in the maritime control system. In 1600, there were about 50 forts between East Africa and Japan. Poor even in European conditions, Portugal could not hope to preserve and profitably maintain such a large and extensive property and to defend It against attacksThe distance problem was an insurmountable obstacle for the commercial and administrative activities in force in the East. While only three weeks were sufficient to cross the Atlantic, the journey to Goa in West India was rarely completed before six months. The round trip from Goa to Macau or Nagasaki ranged from 18 months to three years. In the late 16th and 17th centuries, ship losses on these long voyages, especially between Lisbon and Goa, were heavy and added to the empire's earnings.

The greatest external challenge to the Portuguese came from their European rivals, particularly the Netherlands. The Dutch East India company was founded in 1602, soon after Dutch merchants financed research business trips in the 1590s. Over the next 60 years, the Dutch forcibly stripped most of the Portuguese's most lucrative mail, especially those dealing with the Spice Islands. The Dutch victory was not only in the military and naval sphere. This success was also commercial. The Dutch quickly emerged as Europe's foremost merchant nation. They captured the largest portion of European shipping and built the world's largest merchant fleet. Therefore

America

European exploration and expansion in the Americas presents a strikingly different picture from what is happening in Africa and Asia. It was there that the arrival of the Europeans had its greatest and most lasting impact. Instead of developing trade with the indigenous people, the Europeans established terrestrial empires and began to settle in the Americas themselves. By 1600, the Portuguese Empire was left with nothing more than a series of islands and forts stretching from West Africa to China. Whereas the Spaniards had already conquered an area in America several times the size of Spain at that time, why was there such an opposition between the two empires?

The answer lies partly in the different forces behind Spanish expansionism, and partly in the very different circumstances encountered in the Americas. As we have seen, the Portuguese empire was a commercial empire born of the sea, rooted in the Portuguese traditions of maritime trade and Atlantic voyages. The customs and appearance of Castilian Spain were quite different.

When Columbus appealed to the Portuguese Court in 1484 with a plan to cross the Atlantic westward to Japan and China, the Portuguese had two reasons for rejecting him. First, they had hitherto focused heavily on African exploration and trade, and their longstanding desire to cross the Indian Ocean.

they were trying to achieve. They were therefore reluctant to delay acquiring the known riches of Asian trade for the sake of an uncertain westward voyage. Second, the Portuguese's geographic knowledge was advanced enough to assess Columbus's very small portrayal of the circumference of the earth and, accordingly, the distance of Europe to Asia from the west. By contrast, Isabella's Spain of Castile was relatively new to the exploration of the Atlantic. As rivals to the Portuguese and late starters, the Castiles had to lose little and probably gain a lot by funding Columbus.

The new landmass, uncovered by Columbus's expeditions, initially provided an unwelcome obstacle to the Spanish ambitions to find a western route to Asia. A way was sought to pass around or over this land mass. While there was a certain curiosity about the size and length of the new continent, the main impetus for the Castilians was the ardent passion for competition with other powers. The Portuguese were known to advance rapidly across the Asian seas. Before the Portuguese arrived in 1500, they had landed on the coast of Brazil in South America. England, through the voyages of John Cabot (Italian sailor in the service of England, discovered the North American mainland in 1497), fishermen from Portugal, England, and France traveled to Newfoundland (a large island in eastern Canada, c. n.

Competition with the Portuguese was sharpened by a series of Papal proclamations, and treaties were made that sought to draw a demarcation line between Spanish and Portuguese interests. The Treaty of Tordesillas in 1494 agreed to separate Columbus's explorations in the west from Portuguese claims to Africa to the east, about 2,000 km from the Cape Verde Islands. (370 leagues) drew an imaginary line running west. This line was actually drawn far enough west to allow the Portuguese to later claim Brazil. In 1514, a Papal proclamation by Leo X granted the Portuguese not only the areas they could conquer in Africa and India, but also any territory they could reach by traveling eastward. This decision was made by the Spaniards,

The Spaniards launched

expeditions from their forward bases on the islands of Hispaniola and Cuba to seek a route to South East Asia. In 1513, Vasco Nuñez de Balboa, a local Spanish leader, crossed the narrow region that formed the Panama Strait to reach the Pacific coast. The continent's narrowness at this point raised hopes that a suitable route could be found around the Americas to the Pacific side. To explore this possibility, an expeditionary group led by Ferdinand Magellan, a Portuguese in the service of Castile, departed from Seville in September 1519. Participated in the Portuguese capture of Malacca in 1511 and probably Magellan, who had visited Molukka, was convinced that the spice islands were located near the west coast of Spanish America. The expedition group endured great hardships and losses in this expedition, which did not actually come true. Magellan was killed in a battle with the islanders in the Philippines in 1521, and the return to Europe was completed by the Spanish second-in-command, Sebastian del Cano. In three years' travel, the world's first voyage by sea showed that this circumnavigation of South America was too far south and also too dangerous for a regular commercial route. This voyage also revealed that the Pacific Ocean was considerably larger than Magellan had anticipated. Starving and despairing sailors, Pacific Ocean' They struggled for about four months to cross it, and during that time they saw only two small islands. This voyage dramatically improved Europeans' knowledge of the other side of the world and, incidentally, allowed the Spanish to claim the Philippines. But it also convincingly demonstrated that America posed an almost insurmountable barrier and would not provide Spain with a spice island route to rival Portugal's.

Even before the voyage of Magellan and del Cano showed America's distance from Asia, the Spaniards had come to see the new continent as a potentially fertile source of wealth and power rather than an irritating obstacle. The appearance of new lands drew people to it. The bustling and land-hungry frontier of the Spanish reconguista swept first to the Caribbean and then to the

It crossed the Atlantic, reaching the American mainland. The need for workers arose because the Spanish conquistadors and immigrants, who despised manual labor, did not want to cultivate the land themselves. The right to employ the natives of certain villages was denied to pioneer immigrants through the granting of encomiendas by the Kingdom of Castile. African slaves soon began to be brought in to increase the number of workers available or to replace natives who had died or were killed during the early phase of Spanish colonialism.

In the Americas, as in Asia and Africa, the Spaniards and Portuguese paid no attention to the rights of the indigenous peoples living in the occupied lands. In these lands, only Christians had a legal right. In Africa and Asia, the Portuguese rarely made any attempt to transform their claims into real possession. But the European settlement in America, following the footsteps of the Spanish Reconquista, had an expansionist character from the very beginning. On his second voyage in 1493, Columbus brought 1,200 Spaniards, including farmers and artisans, to resettle the islands of Hispaniola. By settling in this area, they hoped to form a self-sufficient community, prospecting for gold, and preparing to further expand Spanish control over the area.The pioneers of territorial expansion in the Americas were the conquistadors (the name given to the Spaniards who conquered Mexico and Peru in the 16th century). Professional conquistadors and The adventurers sought wealth and land for themselves, although they claimed to be acting on behalf of the Spanish monarchs. Feelings of personal passivity were reinforced through religious beliefs and moral superiority over the natives. Bernal Diaz, who wrote the history of the Spanish conquest of Mexico, summed up the conquistadors' aims as follows: "To serve God and His Majesty, to give light and enrichment to those in darkness."

The Conquistadors' greatest hope of wealth rested on acquiring gold, the most tangible and desirable form of power and wealth they could imagine. When Columbus returned to Spain in 1493, he reported seeing evidence of gold on the islands and hoped that much more would be found. This hope was the strongest of all motives for further research, as it was for the Portuguese in Africa. Within 20 years of Columbus' first voyage, all of the Caribbean's principal islands had been stripped of their gold. A substantial amount of gold was found. But the Spaniards' appetite was insatiable. Finally, they turned their attention to the mainland. "El Dorado" (legendary treasure city in South America, sought after by early Spanish explorers, ch.) and what they heard about the rich civilizations of the interior encouraged them. While "El Dorado" meant, in the explorers' time, the land of imaginary riches, the conquistadors attributed the term to a king, a man covered with gold, whose body was supposedly covered with gold dust before bathing in a sacred lake during an annual ceremony. Once again, myths rather than facts determined the character of European expansionism. A frantic search for gold, Spanish in Central America and northern South America Once again, myths rather than facts determined the character of European expansionism. A frantic search for gold, Spanish in Central America and northern South America Once again, myths rather than facts determined the character of European expansionism. A frantic search for gold, Spanish in Central America and northern South America explains both the speed and greed of his research and conquests. Between 1520 and 1550, Spanish adventurers crossed the Andes, advanced by the river south into the Amazon region, and entered modern-day Argentina and Ğili. They explored Florida north and reached the lower Mississippi basin. Ultimately, they did not manage to discover huge amounts of gold, but their search quickly provided information about the geography of these regions to be shown on maps of Europe.

Behind the Spanish conquest of Mexico and Peru lies the quest for gold, land, and personal fame. In 1519, an expeditionary group of about 600 men, under Hernando Cortes, arrived from Cuba to the coast of the Gulf of Mexico. By fighting, using diplomacy, and bluffing, according to his place, he reached from the jungles of the coastal jungle to the high plateau of central Mexico and the Aztec capital of Tenochtitlan (modern Mexico City). Despite their small numbers, the Spaniards captured Emperor Montezuma. They neutralized Aztec forces in the capital and finally established Spanish rule in central Mexico after defeating Montezuma's successor in

August 1921. This important achievement of Cortes and his soldiers was a second conquistadors, Francisco Pizarro in 1531. He also mobilized with a force of less than 150 men against the Inca Empire in the Peruvian Andes. Within two years, the Inca Emperor Atahualpa was captured and executed, and his empire was annexed to Spain.

How did so few Europeans conquer such a vast and populous empire? Spaniards in Africa and Asia Unlike the Portuguese, they did not find an existing commercial system that they could inherit from the Americas or even partially control. Although they briefly exchanged necklaces for gold on the Gulf coast, it was not a limited coastal trade that attracted them but the prospect of conquest and plundering of these territories, driven by the rumor of a rich inland region. Also, despite their small numbers, those who launched the offensive were convinced of the superiority of their religion and European civilization. This has led them to be generally determined and agile in achieving their goals.Indigenous peoples living in Central America and northern South America were technically and psychologically unprepared to resist the decisive attacks of the Europeans. While the Mexican stone axes and fire-hardened arrowheads could inflict mortal wounds, they were no match for the steel swords and cannons of Cortes' forces. These powerful weapons, along with Spanish horses (horses were previously unknown in Mexico) helped the invaders triumph in several key conflicts. The psychological advantages of firearms and horses were greater than their purely military usefulness. The dominant attitudes of the Spaniards frightened the natives and undermined their confidence in their ability to triumph. Montezuma himself was indecisive and did not know how to react to the Spaniards. Them, He was in a dilemma as to whether to see them as dangerous enemies to be kept as far away as possible, or as gods, as had been suggested. Cortés, out of this indecision of the emperor, disobeyed his orders to stay ashore, then befriended him in Tenochtitlan, and threw him into the hands of the Spaniards.

He deftly took advantage of it, trapping him in being a real puppet ruler in his hands. On the other hand, other factors, such as the unwitting Spanish introduction of a disease into Mexico, the outbreak of a smallpox epidemic, further strengthened the invaders' advantage by demoralizing the natives and making them suspicious of their god's power against the Spanish Christians. The pace of Mexican and Peruvian invasions and the great technological and cultural gap between Europeans and Native Americans did not allow Native Americans to recover from the shock of European intervention, devise effective methods of resistance, and acquire horses and firearms. Much later, when the natives of the North American plains had these innovations,

On the other hand, the invaders also took advantage of two main weaknesses of the Aztec and Inca Empires. Since these empires were centralized states under a single emperor, with the capture of the emperor and the capture of the capitals, the Spanish conquistadors were able to actually seize, or at least temporarily neutralize, the powers of the state. The second weakness lay in the spread of lands to very distant areas. The Aztecs and Incas had created disgruntled elements and hostile adversaries in the frontier areas of their empires. They were easily won over by the invaders and used as military allies, carriers, guides, and spies, as were the peoples on the coast and east of Mexico. The acquisition of native collaborators, the numericalHe remedied his weaknesses and led them to provide collaborators with information about this country and its people that would allow it to wage a more effective fight against its main enemies. In Peru, the capacity of the Incas to resist Spanish invaders was further weakened by the recent civil war and the continued indecision of Emperor Atahualpa.

The period of the Conquistadors, though dramatic and devastating, was short-lived. After this period, the Spaniards, from their bases in Mexico and Peru, began longer attempts to subjugate the other peoples of Central and South America. It took decades, in some cases, to achieve this goal. The Conquistadors also quarreled with each other over the sharing of the spoils of conquest. But the real winner from the conquests was the Kingdom of Castile. However, the kingdom did not seem ready to establish for itself a strong and semi-independent noble state in the New World as it had once done in Spain. A Spanish Governor was appointed in 1535, thus starting imperial rule. Although the search for El Dorado continued sporadically, Spanish Americans they now turned to more determined occupations. The indigenous agricultural activities of maize, potatoes and other vegetable crops were threatened by the introduction of large-scale farming from Spain's own rural areas. The number of demoralized natives surviving after the Conquest was dwarfed by disease and forced labor. Central Mexico's population had fallen from about 25 million at the time of the conquest to one million in 1600. The heavy pressure exerted by the traditional forms of conquest and worship It was greatly diminished by diseases and forced labor. Central Mexico's population had fallen from about 25 million at the time of the conquest to one million in 1600. The heavy pressure exerted by the traditional forms of conquest and worship It was greatly diminished by diseases and forced labor. Central Mexico's population had fallen from about 25 million at the time of the conquest to one million in 1600. The heavy pressure exerted by the traditional forms of conquest and worship

It led to faster progress than in Africa and Asia. Between 1524 and 1536, about 4 million conversions were recorded in Mexico alone.

Although the Conquistadors were disappointed in their dreams of El Dorado, the Spaniards discovered rich silver deposits in Zacatecas, Mexico, and the Patasi region of modern-day Bolivia in the 1540s. Instead of the gold that inspired conquests and exploration, silver quickly became a real source of American mineral wealth.

Apart from all its benefits to Europe's own economy, silver led to the expansion of Europe's spice and textile trade with Asia. The era of a European world economy had begun to emerge.

Conclusion

Historians are less inclined today than in the past to view the Age of Discovery as the result of a sudden advance in European technology or the success of a few individuals who almost single-handedly pioneered ocean exploration. Instead, they view the travels and conquests of the 15th and 16th centuries as the result of economic, cultural, and technological developments that have begun to mature in Europe since at least the 11th and 12th centuries. To say this is not to deny the importance of any personal initiative. Because the imagination, courage and determination of people like Prince Henry, Dias, Da Gama, Columbus, Magellan, Cortes and Pizarro,

It accelerated the development of European expansionism and helped determine its character and direction. But they relied on an existing foundation while raising the knowledge, skills, resources and passions of the Europeans to a higher level. So it seems certain that other European sailors and adventurers would eventually have done all this if Columbus had not crossed the Atlantic in 1492 and Cortes had not captured Mexico in 1521. In the travels of the Vikings, the wars and conquests of the Crusaders, and the commercial activities of the Genoese and Venetians, Europe made its first attempts at expansionism. However, they failed to achieve a fully mature expansionism. because

Before the 15th century, the maritime technology, resources, and sustaining driving forces needed for systematic research and overseas expansion were not yet available in Europe. The most distinctive feature of the Age of Discovery in the 15th and 16th centuries was the more general European concern with the unity of the Iberian initiative. Portugal and Castile Spain were endowed with a uniquely crusader spirit and had an ideal geographical location for ocean exploration. But Europe as a whole, under the leadership of Italy, contributed to the development of navigation and cartography, the provision of necessary financial support, and the marketing of spices, gold and other products brought to Europe by Iberian ships. Particularly Iberian factors affect Portugal and Castile. He made the leader of expansionism; but those who continued and expanded the expansionist process after 1600, especially The other, including the Netherlands, England, and France

Trying to

explain why the Age of Discovery began at that time and in Europe, modern historians have looked to other civilizations and tried to understand why they did not act before, trying to catch up with and surpass the Europeans. The relatively narrow technological distance between Europe and China, India and the Muslim world in the 15th and 16th centuries is now better known than before. Even in Africa and the Americas, where the technological distance is clearly enormous, historians speak less confidently of the advantages of using firearms on European ships and indigenous peoples. It is now clear that Europeans in many parts of the world do not have the financial strength and resources to impose their will on others

Basically, the advantages of Europe were threefold. Its expanding economy and the importance of its ties to trade provided a constant impetus and determination to his overseas adventures. The experience of political rivalries and warfare within Europe, combined with intermittent conflicts with Islam, gave Europe's travelers and adventurers an additional sense of confidence and aggression. Few states outside of Europe have had such a powerful combination of economic motivation and religious-cultural self-reliance. It was this combination that ensured the Europeans' determination to succeed despite often adverse conditions. China, possibly the largest of Europe's potential competitors, is economically and

It was in stark contrast to his cultural self-sufficiency. This characteristic of him led to an attitude of seeing foreign trade and foreign peoples as petty and worthless, instead of commercial and cultural sociability in the European style. A flourishing spirit of inquiry and a rational approach to problem solving were among the distinctive driving forces of Europe. But superstition, fantasy, and adherence to past authorities were not dead, and more so as Europeans overcame their capacity to research and explore geographic, nautical, and technical problems through trial and error and finding practical solutions.

Equipped with these essential features, Europe was able to take advantage of the local conditions it faced. In some places, such as the Americas,

Europeans took advantage of being surprise enemies in their attacks on indigenous populations. In the Indian Ocean, the surprise was less and the counteraction more effective. But the Europeans found local hostilities to exploit, captured bases; they won naval victories that gave them sufficient leverage to realize their commercial and political ambitions. These early bridgeheads gradually expanded through persistence and seizing opportunities. Not fully equipped with the resources to capitalize on its successes in Asia, Portugal was replaced after 1600 by the Netherlands and England to develop their own commercial and continental empires.

Between 1400 and 1600 was a period of study and exploration, exploration of the oceans, the opening of new trade routes, and the beginning of overseas empires. After 1600, especially under Dutch and English rule,

maritime exploration came to be seen as less important than the consolidation of existing trade routes and the development of new ones. The gold and spice trade, which first encouraged Portuguese ships to sail beyond the rough waters of Cape Bojador, was later joined by new trades such as slaves, sugar, silver, cotton textiles, coffee and tea, and to some extent replaced gold and spices. This wealth from overseas trade helped finance and help build further empires in the Americas and Asia. This wealth also contributed, directly or indirectly, through the further development of capitalism and the industrial revolution, to the western imperialism of the 19th and 20th centuries, which left almost no untouched area in the world.

THE

END